MW01094702

Kim's Travel Guide for RV and Tent Camping in the USA

Coast to Coast Southern Route:
California to Florida

By Kimberly Wiedemeier

Sara Scott, Assistant Editor
Daria Lacy, Layout Production

Other titles by Kimberly Wiedemeier will soon be available through select online retailers:

Kim's Travel Guide for RV and Tent Camping in the USA West Coast Route: California, Oregon and Washington

and

Kim's Travel Guide for RV and Tent Camping in the USA Western Parks Loop: CA, AZ, NM, CO, WY, and MT

License Notes

CONTENTS

ROUTE MAP

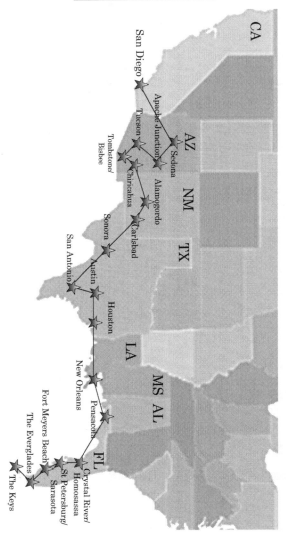

Kim's Travel Guide for RV and Tent Camping in the USA

INTRODUCTION

This step-by-step cross-country travel itinerary is designed to make your trip planning frustration a thing of the past, saving you time and research while on your next adventure. This guide introduces you to the majestic parks, roadside attractions, historic sites, and natural wonders of the southern United States via an easy-to-follow travel itinerary built just for you. Each destination includes RV and tent (as well as cabin, cottage, and bungalow) camping for those traveling on a shoestring budget. I have also included several free campgrounds at many of the destinations on your route.

The Coast to Coast Southern Route includes southern California, Arizona, New Mexico, southern Texas, Louisiana, and Florida (through the southern tip of the Florida Keys). Many of the must-see destinations included here are ones I have personally visited and highly recommend. Others were researched extensively and are included to give you a greater variety of options. As each traveler is unique, it is up to you to decide how far to drive each day, what you wish to see, and how much time you have for your personal adventure.

For those looking for upscale hotels and high-end restaurants, this is not the guide for you. If you are driving an RV or are planning on tent camping most of the way— this is the guide for you! The destinations in this itinerary are suitable for anyone with a love of nature mixed with a little history and culture. The goal is to provide you with the most scenic and budget-friendly camping spots, as well as recreational opportunities and unique diversions along the route.

The section below entitled ESSENTIALS AND TID-BITS, will ensure that you bring those often-forgotten items, rendering your trip a smoother, more comfortable and enjoyable one. Most importantly, take your time, don't sweat the small stuff, and enjoy yourself while driving through this expansive, beautiful and diverse country. The journey can be as exciting as the destination.

ESSENTIALS AND TID-BITS

I recommend making the most of your trip (and your sanity) by driving no more than four to six hours a day. Driving long distances can be tiresome and stressful, so take your time. Road trips also put a significant number of miles, and strain, on your vehicle. Vehicle breakdowns and flat tires can and do happen. Be prepared! Always have a gallon of water (and perhaps engine coolant) available in case you overheat on steep mountain passes. Engine oil is helpful if you have an older vehicle that requires extra lubrication for the long haul. A spare tire and tire-changing tools are also indispensable when you are in the middle of no-man's land. A road atlas is the most reliable source of information for locating free rest stops (Rest stops—especially in Texas—can be excellent overnight RV camping spots. Many offer free Wifi, playgrounds, and interpretive trails.)

Pets (i.e., well-behaved dogs) are allowed in most public campgrounds as long as they are leashed. Some private RV parks have strict pet policies, and these will be noted as "No pets" in the Camping section of this travel guide.

Be prepared for any type of weather. Bring clothing and shoes suitable for rain, snow, wind, and heat. You never know when the weather will turn. It's a good idea to bring a hat and gloves (even during warm camping seasons). Bring a swimsuit for ocean dips and waterfall plunges. Sticky bottomed water shoes are great for tidepool walks, and flip-flop sandals are essential after a day of hiking (and for wearing in public showers). An umbrella will save the day when walking through unpredictably rainy cities like New Orleans. Bring a string or clothesline (and clothespins) for hanging wet or washed clothing and swimsuits overnight.

Many campgrounds take cash, credit, and personal checks. I have found that a good number of campgrounds (especially self-serve) do NOT take credit cards, so be sure to have cash or personal checks available for nightly stays. Rolls of quarters are a must for campground showers. Most coin operated showers cost between $1.50 and $3.00 for a timed shower.

Having a source of outdoor lighting in the evenings is important when you're RV or tent camping. Bring a lantern (with extra batteries) for cooking and washing dishes outdoors, and a headlamp for nighttime bathroom trips and reading in bed. To note, in muggy places like Florida, mosquitoes and no-see-ums (tiny biting flies) come out at dusk. A lightweight bug shelter (a tent with see-through mesh) will be a lifesaver in the evenings!

Camera batteries usually last about a week. Bring a battery charger and appropriate adapter for cameras and cell phones to keep your essential media working.

Have a corkscrew or bottle opener on hand for that much-needed, end-of-day libation, as well as a can opener for those convenient, quick canned suppers. Refillable water bottles and bladders are convenient while on the road and on long day hikes.

Comfortable chairs (particularly lounging types) are indispensable for hanging out near your camper or tent on comfortable evenings, as well as for stargazing! You will likely need a day or two per week to relax, read, and recuperate from your non-stop adventures. A lounge chair overlooking the countryside will provide some of your best memories.

Most importantly, create a running list of things to bring prior to your departure. It is no fun trying to remember everything last minute or having to turn the RV around! Here is a run-down of the items I've mentioned above:

gallon of water	**lantern**
engine coolant	**extra batteries**
engine oil	**headlamp**
spare tire/tools	**bug shelter**
hat and gloves	**battery charger/adapter**
swimsuit	**bottle opener**
water shoes	**water bottle/bladder**
flip flops	**lounge chairs**
umbrella	**books**
clothesline	**road atlas**
roll of quarters	**cash or checks**

COAST TO COAST SOUTHERN ROUTE— HERE WE GO!

This travel itinerary will begin in southern California's city of San Diego and take us east across the southern states to the Florida Keys. Each stop will include recommendations for camping and must-see local attractions. For reference, each destination on the route shows the travel time (in hours) from the previous location on the itinerary.

CALIFORNIA

San Diego, CA

SAN DIEGO

La Jolla Cove, San Diego

CAMPING

South Carlsbad State Beach (7201 Carlsbad Blvd, Carls-bad) – Located 40 minutes north of downtown San Diego, this campground offers over 200 RV and tent sites on a bluff near the ocean. Full RV hookups, dump station, re-strooms with showers, drinking water, fire pits (firewood available), and camp store on-site. Advanced reservations recommended. Fees: Tent and RV (35' max length) $35-$50 (depending on site location). Park phone: (760) 438-3143. Book at www.reserveamerica.com.

San Elijo State Beach (2050 South Coast Highway 101, Encinitas) – Located 20 minutes north of downtown San Diego, this campground offers over 170 RV and tent sites overlooking the Pacific. Full RV hookups, dump station, drinking water, showers, fire pits (firewood available), camp store and snack bar on-site. Advanced reservations recommended. Fees: Tent $35-$50, RV (35' max length) $60-$75. Park phone: (760) 753-5091. Book at www.reserveamerica.com.

Campland on the Bay (2211 Pacific Beach Drive, San Diego) – This urban RV park is in the central Mission Bay area of San Diego. The campground offers family activities, a private beach, two swimming pools, laundry, showers, free Wifi, a fitness center and café. Tent camping is available but not ideal here. Campsites range from dry to bay view to private VIP sites (with their own jacuzzi and private entry). Price ranges are reflective of the seasons. Fees: RV (no length limit) $45 (dry)-$225 (VIP). Reservations can be made at 1 (800) 4-BAY-FUN (800-422-9386) or online at www.campland.com/reservations.

Chula Vista RV Resort (460 Sandpiper Way, Chula Vista) – This lovely and well-maintained RV park is located just 20 minutes south of downtown San Diego, directly on South San Diego Bay. It is adjacent to a 552-slip marina, a grassy park with playground and walking paths, and an attractive waterfront restaurant. Amenities include a pool/jacuzzi, fitness room, general store, laundry, full RV hookups, pull-thru sites, and privacy landscaping. Rates: RV (no length limit) $91-$123 daily (depending on site and season). No tent camping available.

Sweetwater Summit Regional Park (3218 Summit Meadow Road, Bonita) – Located 20 minutes southeast of downtown San Diego, this inland campground provides 112 tent and RV sites with full hookups, modern restrooms with showers, and BBQ grills (firewood available). Recreation includes hiking, mountain biking, fishing at the nearby Sweetwater Reservoir, and a small aquatic water park and playground on-site. Fees: Tent $24, RV (45' max length) $29-$33. Call (619) 472-7572 for reservations.

Barona Casino (1932 Wildcat Canyon Road, Lakeside) – Located 30 minutes east of downtown San Diego, the casino provides free RV dry camping in a small fenced parking area; no amenities. Check in with the security office or call in advance for availability at (619) 443-2300. Free.

MUST-SEE ATTRACTIONS

La Jolla Cove (1100 Coast Blvd, La Jolla) – Walking along this oceanfront park provides spectacular views, abundant marine life (harbor seals, sea lions, pelicans and cormorants, and brightly colored fish), and opportunities for snorkeling and kayaking in the sea caves. There are many great ocean-view restaurants within walking distance of the cove.

San Diego Zoo (2920 Zoo Drive, San Diego) – Famous for its rare and unique tropical gardens and aviaries, a renowned panda exhibit, and an aerial tram overlooking downtown San Diego. This 100-acre park, with over 800 species of animals, is not to be missed. Admission: Adult $52, Child (age 3-11) $42, Children under 3 (Free)

Torrey Pines State Natural Reserve (12600 North Torrey Pines Road, La Jolla) – This park encompasses eight miles of coastal trails atop a rugged seaside bluff and along the pristine coastline. The beach is great for surfing or sunbathing and is often not crowded during the weekdays. Free parking is available along the coastline if you grab a spot early; north and south parking lots charge $10-$20 (dependent on the season).

Balboa Park (1549 El Prado Street, San Diego) – The historic Spanish-Renaissance style buildings at this city park house numerous museums, an artist colony, an arboretum, spectacular rose and desert gardens, and the world-famous San Diego Zoo. Free entry to all the gardens, art colony, arboretum, and the elegant Timkin Art Museum. Admission fee for all other museums and the zoo.

Balboa Park arboretum, San Diego

Hotel Del Coronado (1500 Orange Avenue, Coronado) – This Victorian-style hotel built in 1888 is one of America's largest wooden structures. Enjoy the pristine beach (if you want to avoid crowds) and keep an eye out for the resident sandcastle builder. Stop at the hotel creamery for a sweet treat and ask the reservations desk if you can walk along the upstairs corridors. The winding, narrow halls have an air of mystery, and two rooms on the 3rd floor are rumored to be haunted.

Old Town San Diego (2482 San Diego Avenue) – Considered the oldest village in California, Old Town is home to a unique mission-era State Park (with many original buildings to explore), numerous curio shops, a pioneer cemetery, and a hub of Mexican restaurants. (La Piñata on Juan Street is my personal favorite.) Some unique stops include Heritage Park Victorian Village (2455 Heritage Park Row, San Diego) and the Mormon Battalion Historic Site. Guides in period costume offer a free, interactive tour suitable for children and adults (2510 Juan Street).

Sunset Cliffs Natural Park (Sunset Cliffs Blvd and Ladera Street intersection, San Diego) – This coastal park provides excellent views while walking along the coastal bluffs. (Look for the stairway leading down to the beach) Explore the intricately carved arches and sea caves, and during low tide you'll find the tidal pools teeming with life. Afterward, take a walk on the nearby Ocean Beach Pier for a late breakfast or lunch at the Pier Café (Sunset Ciffs Bvd and Niagara Ave—walk west until you get to the end of the pier).

Torrey Pines Glider Port (2800 Torrey Pines Scenic Drive, La Jolla) – Watch the paragliders and hang gliders launch over the cliffs while sipping a drink on the rooftop deck of the cafe. Be sure to go on a relatively windy day to see the most gliders. For the avid hiker, there is a well maintained (albeit steep) trail next to the port that leads to one of San Diego's best surfing beaches.

Seaport Village (849 W. Harbor Drive, San Diego) – Located on the waterfront adjacent to Downtown San Diego, the Village is an excellent stop for a stroll along the harbor, perusing artisan shops, and dining at the waterfront cafes. On weekends there are street performers and, in summer, regular concerts on the bay. For the late-nighter, take a stroll to downtown's Gaslamp District and visit the fun pubs and restaurants, people watch, and admire the historic architecture.

ARIZONA

| Sedona | Apache Junction | Tucson | Tombstone/Bisbee | Chiricahua |

SEDONA

6.5 hours east of San Diego, CA

Cathedral Rocks, Sedona

Note: Sedona is one of the most beautiful geologic areas in Arizona. Stop at the South Gateway Visitor Center on Hwy 179 for road and trail maps, as well as the $15 vehicle Red Rock Pass—good for parking/hiking/camping in dispersed wilderness areas.

CAMPING

Manzanita Campground (Hwy 89A, six miles north of Sedona) – This 19-site campground is open year-round for tent and small vehicle camping only. It is located on Oak Creek within scenic Oak Creek Canyon. Bathrooms, drinking water, BBQ grills, fire pits (firewood available), fishing and swimming on-site. Fees: Tent $22. Park phone: (928) 204-2034. Book early at www.reserveamerica.com.

Cave Springs Campground (Hwy 89A, nine miles north of Sedona) – Open Spring-Fall, Cave Springs is an 84-site RV and tent campground located within scenic Oak Creek Canyon. Vault restrooms, showers, BBQ grills, fire pits, and drinking water on-site; no RV hookups. Fishing and seasonal swimming allowed. Fees: Tent and RV (36' max length) $22. Park phone: (928) 282-1629. Book early at www.reserveamerica.com.

Camp Avalon (91 Loy Lane, Sedona) – Open year around, Camp Avalon is located 10 minutes from downtown Sedona along serene Oak Creek. It is a privately owned spiritual retreat center that allows private campers on its property. Fresh drinking water and porta-potties available (no other amenities); only small to medium-sized RVs and trailers can be accommodated. Fees: $25 per day for two people ($10 for each additional person). Book online at www.avalon.camp or text the Camp Manager at (928) 301-3917 to arrange check-in.

Rancho Sedona RV Park (135 Bear Wallow Lane, Sedona) – This full-service, all-season RV park (no tent camping) is nestled within a sycamore shaded area with spacious RV sites, and is within walking distance to local shopping and restaurants. Free Wifi, cable TV, and laundry facilities on-site. Fees: RV (by length; no limit) $36-$69. Reservations must be made by phone at (888) 641-4261.

Loy Butte Road (FR 525) and Sycamore Pass Road (525C) Primitive Camping (10 miles south of downtown Sedona, turn off Hwy 89A onto FR 525/Loy Butte Road).

– Note: GPS directions will take you down Boynton Pass Road to get to FR 525—do not take this longer unpaved route unless you are highly adventurous! Dispersed camping is allowed the first five miles of FR 525/Loy Butte Road, starting at the intersection of Hwy 89A; camping is also allowed on all of FR 525C (which intersects FR 525 four miles in). Vehicles with decent clearance are recommended on both roads (though I have safely driven a sedan on FR 525). Red Rock Pass required.

Oak Creek Canyon, Sedona

MUST-SEE ATTRACTIONS

V-Bar-V Ranch Rock Art Heritage Site (6750 N Forest Ranger Road, Rimrock) – Just SE of Sedona (off FR 618), this fascinating and unspoiled Indian rock art site is located ½ mile up an easy, oak-lined trail. It requires a volunteer guide, whom can be found in the small ranch-style building near the parking lot. Open 9:30 a.m.– 3:00 p.m., Fri–Mon; gate closes at 3:00 p.m. Red Rock Pass required. Note: There is a great swimming hole located under the bridge, about two miles before V-Bar-V Ranch on FR 618.

Courthouse Butte Loop Trail (Bell Rock Vista parking lot, Hwy 179 (milepost 309.8), Sedona) – This easy to moderate trail (four miles round trip) gets you up close and personal with the gorgeous red rock sandstone formations of Sedona. Start your hike on the Bell Rock Pathway (trailhead at parking lot) until you see the intersection with Courthouse Butte Loop Trail. A Red Rock Pass can be obtained at the trailhead kiosk.

West Fork of Oak Creek Trail (Hwy 89A, 9.5 miles north of Sedona, at Call O' the Canyon day-use area) – This gorgeous trail meanders along year-around Oak Creek, with narrow passages surrounded by eroding sandstone cliffs. You will cross an historic ruin and well-hidden Indian rock art along the way (six miles round trip). Look for the West Fork trailhead sign and turn down the paved road that ends at Call O' The Canyon day-use parking lot. Day use fee: $10

Palatki/Honanki Ruins (Boynton Pass Road to FR 795) Palatki is home to 1000 year-old Sinagua cliff dwellings and pictographs—some of the best in the Sedona area. Take 89A south (from downtown Sedona) three miles to Dry Creek Road. Turn right. Go three miles to stop sign. Turn left. When you get to Enchantment Resort go left at fork (Boynton Pass Road/FR 152C). The road becomes dirt here. Drive four miles to junction of FR 525. Turn right, then in .1 mile take another right at FR 795. Drive 1.8 miles to the Palatki parking area. To explore more ancient ruins, visit the very sizable Honanki just a few miles further down FR 525 (signs will be posted).

Airport Mesa "Vortex" (Airport Road, Sedona—look for the dirt parking area on the left, about two-thirds the way up Airport Road) – This short 200-yard hike takes you to Sedona's famous "energy vortex", a magnetic anomaly in the earth. It also offers amazing 360-degree views of the red rock landscape. Afterwards, visit the airport café (Mesa Grill) at the top of Airport Road. It offers good food and even better views.

Historic Mining Town of Jerome (Hwy 89A, Jerome) – Considered "the largest ghost town in America" and only 20 miles south of Sedona, this quaint town sits vertically atop narrow, winding Cleopatra Hill. The top of the hill offers local artisan shops and galleries, historic sites, kitschy restaurants, and the infamously haunted Jerome Grand Hotel. Jerome is a fun, optional drive when heading south of Sedona toward our next stop—Apache Trail.

APACHE TRAIL (SR 88)

3 hours southeast of Sedona

Apache Trail viewpoint, Arizona

Note: Located 45 minutes east of Phoenix, SR 88 is a hidden gem of canyons and lakes, great hiking, and sizable ghost towns within high desert canyon country. The road is paved, windy and narrow for approximately 22 miles (max. vehicle length 40'), with the historic stage stop town of Tortilla Flat at mile 17. If your vehicle allows, continue on the unpaved (well-graded) portion through steep-walled canyon country for another 22 miles. Note: the unpaved section of SR 88 has hairpin turns and single lane sections, and it will take several hours to complete the trail. There is excellent camping and photo opportunities along the way. Once you reach Roosevelt Lake, the road is paved again (SR 188). From here, take SR 188 south to Hwy 10 and our next stop—Tucson

CAMPING

Lost Dutchman State Park (6109 N. Apache Trail, Apache Junction) – This full-service, 134-site RV and tent campground offers the Superstition Mountains as its stunning backdrop, as well as several hiking trails and a sizable ghost town to explore. This is a great overnight stop before (or after) a day of exploring the Apache Trail and historic Tortilla Flat. Fees: Park entry $7, Tent $15-20, RV (80' max length) $25-$30. Reservation line: (520) 586-2283. Online: www.azstateparks.com.

Canyon Lake Marina Campground (16802 N.E. Highway 88, Tortilla Flat) – This scenic lakeside campground is 15 miles up the paved portion of SR 88. It offers 28 RV and 19 tent sites. Recreation includes small boat rentals, paddlewheel boat tours, fishing, swimming and hiking. Full RV hookups, showers, drinking water, BBQ grills, fire pits (firewood available), and an on-site restaurant. No dump station (though pump-outs can be scheduled for a $20 fee). Fees: Tent $30-$35, RV (30' max length) $55-$60. Call (480) 288-9233 for reservations.

Tortilla Campground (17 miles up SR 88 at Tortilla Flat) – This 76-site campground, located at historic Tortilla Flat, is nestled in the Superstition Mountain range surrounded by saguaro cactus and red rock vistas. Amenities include restrooms with flush toilets, drinking water, fire pits with grills, and an RV dump station; no RV hookups. Fees: RV (22' max length) and tent $12 at fee kiosk. Call Tonto Basin Ranger District for availability: (928) 467-3200.

Burnt Corral Campground (SR 88 at mile 42 near Roosevelt Dam) – This rustic 82-site campground overlooks beautiful Apache Lake. It is ideal for tent campers or small RVs under 40' since it is located on the unpaved portion of SR 88. It offers 12 RV pull-thru sites (no hookups), vault toilets and drinking water. Fees: RV (max length 40') and tent $12 at fee kiosk (first come). Call Tonto Basin Ranger District for availability: (928) 467-3200.

Oak Flat Campground (FR 469/Magma Mine Road off Hwy 60 near Superior, AZ) – This is a convenient, free dry camping area following a day's drive along the Apache Trail (and continuing south on to Globe, AZ). Rustic campsites are scattered among cedar and live oak. Vault toilets available; no water. The campground offers 14 RV pull-thru sites and 16 tent sites. Look for campground signs at Hwy 60 and Magma Mine Road. Free.

MUST-SEE ATTRACTIONS

Tortilla Flat (17 miles up SR 88, Tortilla Flat) – This famous historic stagecoach stop is only a 1/2 block long but offers a quaint museum, gift shop, mercantile store, and Mexican cantina. The kitschy saloon displays dollar bill covered walls, horse saddle seats, and offers tasty chili pepper beer. There is excellent camping across the highway (see Camping).

Canyon Lake Tour (15 miles up SR 88 at Canyon Lake Marina) – Steep canyon walls follow Canyon Lake's 20 miles of incredible, winding water passages. It is common to see bighorn sheep on the surrounding cliffs. Rent a small outboard motor boat at the marina or take a 90-minute cruise on the Dolly Steamboat ($23). The Lakeside Restaurant and Cantina offers excellent food and views of the lake canyon.

Boulder Canyon Trail (just across SR 88 from Canyon Lake Marina, see Camping) – This strenuous, yet gorgeous, hike gives you panoramic views of Canyon Lake and the Superstition ridge line, including Weaver's Needle and aptly named Battleship Mountain (seven miles round trip).

Tonto National Monument (26260 N Hwy 188, Roosevelt) – Tonto National Monument offers a glimpse into ancient Sinagua Indian life via a self-guided trail to cliff dwellings overlooking Roosevelt Lake. The three-mile, ranger-led hike to the Upper Cliff Dwellings requires advanced reservations (Nov–April). Call (928) 467-2241 to reserve a free spot on the hike (all skill levels welcomed).

Tonto National Monument, Arizona

TUCSON

2.5 hours from Apache Trail, AZ

Catalina Scenic Byway, Tucson

CAMPING

Gilbert Ray Campground/Tucson Mountain Park (Gates Pass Road, Tucson) – This first-come, first-served tent and RV campground is located just five miles from Saguaro National Park within the beautiful Sonoran Desert. 135 campsites, full RV hookups, dump station, restrooms and drinking water available. Fees: Tent $10, RV (36' max length) $20 at the self-pay kiosk. Park phone: (520) 877-6000.

Catalina State Park (11570 N. Oracle Road, Tucson) – This year-around campground offers 120 tent and RV sites with full hookups. Amenities include dump station, modern restrooms with showers, BBQ grills, gift shop and Visitor Center. Recreation includes hiking, biking and volunteer-guided nature walks. Fees: Park entry $7, Tent $15-$20, RV (no length limit) $20-$30. Online reservations recommended at www.azstateparks.com. Park phone: (520) 628-5798.

Molino Basin Campground (Catalina Hwy off Tanque Verde Road; between mileposts 5 and 6) – Open November to early May, this 34-site tent and RV campground is located 10 miles up the beautiful and winding Catalina Scenic Byway (a.k.a. General Hitchcock Hwy) north of Tucson. No hookups or water available. Vault toilets and picnic tables on-site. Fees: Tent and RV (22' max length) $10 at self-pay kiosk. Call Santa Catalina Ranger District for availability (520) 749-8700.

Rose Canyon Campground (Catalina Hwy/Rose Canyon Road, Tucson) – Open April through October, this 67-site tent and RV campground is located 13 miles up the beautiful and winding Catalina Scenic Byway (a.k.a. General Hitchcock Hwy) in a cool mixed forest near Rose Canyon Lake. Vault toilets and drinking water available; no hookups. Fees: Tent and RV (22' max length) $22 at self-pay kiosk. Call Santa Catalina Ranger District for availability (520) 749-8700.

Snyder Hill BLM Road (Hwy 86 and S. South Joaquin Road, Tucson) – Dispersed camping on BLM land just off Hwy 86 (a.k.a. Ajo Hwy) and S. San Joaquin Road, seven miles west of Tucson. It offers convenient, overnight boondocking when full-service camping isn't available. Just look for the fire rings and other boondocked RVs. Free.

Casino Del Sol (5655 West Valencia Road, Tucson) – This large Tucson casino allows overnight RV parking in its expansive parking lot. No amenities. Free.

MUST-SEE ATTRACTIONS

Saguaro National Park (West Entrance-2700 N. Kinney Road, Tucson; East Entrance-3693 S. Old Spanish Trail, Tucson) – This park is famous for its towering saguaro cactus, sweeping mountain landscapes, and excellent mountain biking and hiking. The park has two Visitor Centers offering park trail maps, ranger-led programs, and exhibits on the cultural and natural history of the Sonoran Desert. Fees: Park entry $10. No camping available.

Sabino Canyon (5900 N. Sabino Canyon Road, Tucson) – This desert oasis offers moderate trails that follow Bear Canyon creek through the Sonoran Desert landscape to the famous Seven Falls (7.8 miles round trip). Bring your swimsuit and lots of water. The canyon can also be viewed via the open-air shuttle bus tour, which departs from the Sabino Canyon Visitor Center several times daily. Fees: Parking $5 per day; Coronado Recreation Pass $5; Bus Tour $10.

Sabino Canyon's Seven Falls, Tucson

Arizona-Sonora Desert Museum (2021 N. Kinney Road, Tucson) – This beautiful desert park is a 98-acre natural history museum, zoo, and botanical garden. It contains two miles of walking paths on 21 acres, 300 animal species and 1,200 kinds of plants. Admission: Adult $21.95, Child (age 3-12) $8.95.

Kartchner Caverns State Park (2980 AZ Hwy 90, Benson) – Kartchner Caverns is a living, growing cave system, offering some of the best cavern tours in Arizona. At a constant 77 degrees, with 99% humidity, the Throne Room and Big Room can be toured throughout the day, each via a 90-minute, ranger-guided walk. Advanced reservations recommended. Call (520) 586-2283 or visit www. azstateparks.com/kartchner/. Fees: Park entry $7; Cavern tours: Adult $23, Child (age 7-13) $13, Child (age 0-6) $5.

TOMBSTONE/BISBEE

2 hours from Tucson, AZ

Main Street Actors, Tombstone

Note: The historic towns of Tombstone and Bisbee, AZ are combined since they can both be seen on a full day excursion, spending about two to three hours at each location depending on your personal interests. Both are unique,

Tombstone being the quintessential Wild West town, and the location of the infamous OK Corral shootout. Bisbee is a historic and colorful mining town, with restored neighborhoods of Victorian and European-style homes perched precariously on the hillside.

CAMPING

Tombstone RV Park and Campground (1475 AZ Hwy 80, Tombstone) – Located one mile from downtown Tombstone, this park offers full hookups and amenities, and is well maintained. Rustic cabins are also available. A shuttle is provided to downtown for overnight guests. Fees: Tent $25, RV (50' max length) $30-$40, Cabins $50. Reservations by phone at (520) 457-3829 or email tombstonervparkcg@gmail.com.

Queen Mine RV Park (473 N Dart Rd, Bisbee) – Bisbee's only in-town RV park with 25 spaces overlooking downtown Bisbee. It is located next to the famous Queen Mine (tours offered). Showers, Wifi and cable TV available. No tent camping. Fees: RV $30. Call (520) 432-5006 for reservations.

Double Adobe Campground and Recreational Ranch (5057 W. Double Adobe Road, McNeal) – This modest, well-maintained private campground is located 10 miles SE of Bisbee. It offers 77 RV spaces and 20 tent sites. Full hookups, laundry and shower facilities available. On-site recreation includes sport shooting (trap, skeet, clay), birding, and billiards. Fees: Tent $16, RV (80' max length) $20-$35. Phone: (520) 364-4000.

MUST-SEE ATTRACTIONS

Boothill Graveyard (408 N. Hwy 80, Tombstone) – This historic graveyard is a bit touristy, but the unique epitaphs offer an intimate look into the rough and tumble lifestyle of those that lived and died in Tombstone. I had a "ghost" sighting here. Maybe you will too! Admission: Adults $3, Children 15 years and younger (Free).

Allen Street – Find a free parking spot anywhere near Allen Street and begin your stroll of historic Tombstone. Visit the historic museums, shops, and restaurants along Allen Street, and watch the impromptu Western-style street performances and hourly gun shootouts.

Big Nose Kate's Saloon and Restaurant (417 E. Allen Street, Tombstone) – Take a peek inside this beautiful National Historic Landmark. Restaurant patrons can get their photos taken with the cowboys and saloon girls for free. Once inside, there is a spiral staircase that takes you down to the original bar (now a boutique shop). Once there, take a peek at the "Swamper's Room" and open the mineshaft door.

The Bird Cage Theater (517 E Allen Street, Tombstone) – Hailed as the wildest and meanest place in Tombstone, ladies-of-the-night entertained patrons of this gambling hall from their "cribs" situated along the walls. It is now a fantastic museum, full of historic artifacts and ghost sightings. Knowledgeable tour guides and special ghost tours offered (recommended). Admission: Self-Guided Tour $10, Ghost Tour $20.

Bisbee Walking Tours (Tours start from the Copper Queen Hotel (11 Howell Avenue) or the Bisbee Visitor Center (#1 Main Street) – The best way to see Bisbee is on foot, meandering the winding streets and climbing its many narrow stairways. Historic and colorful Victorian homes perch precariously on the hillsides. The Copper Queen Hotel offers a self-guided tour map; the Bisbee

Visitor Center offers walking and driving tours for a nominal fee.

Queen Mine Tour (478 North Dart Road, Bisbee) – Suit up and take the historic mine car a lengthy 1,500 feet down into the Queen Copper Mine. Local miner-turned-tour guides expertly narrate the way. The tour is approximately 1 hour 15 minutes. Five daily tours offered. Admission: Adult $13, Child (age 6-12) $5.50, Children under age 6 not permitted underground. Call (866) 432-2071 to make a reservation (often not necessary).

CHIRICAHUA NATIONAL MONUMENT
2 hours from Bisbee, AZ (Hwy 181)

Spire formations, Chiricahua National Monument

Note: This wonderland of rocks is not to be missed, and it is a fee-free park. The Chiricahua spires are comprised of volcanic "tuff", creating a majestic geologic landscape of pinnacles and grottoes. The park can be icy in the winter (Dec-March), being situated at 5,400 ft and upwards to 7,000 ft, so use caution. Obtain gas in Willcox, 35 miles from the park, as there are no gas stations within the park.

CAMPING

Bonita Canyon Campground (within Chiricahua National Monument, Hwy 181 to E Bonita Canyon Rd, Willcox) – This 26-site campground is situated in a shady pine and oak forest surrounded by Chiricahua's unique geologic formations. Gray water dump station, bathrooms and water available; no hookups. Fees: Tent and RV (29' max length) $20. Reservations can be made at www.recreation.gov.

Pinery Canyon Road (FR 42) – Usually open April-November (7,000 ft elevation), this gravel road is suitable for passenger vehicles with decent clearance. FR 42 is located just before the entrance to Chiricahua National Monument; turn right (south) on Pinery Canyon Road and drive approximately four miles to the free primitive sites (look for fire rings). Note: Pinery Canyon Campground is seven miles further, but no need to go that far for legal primitive camping.

MUST-SEE ATTRACTIONS

Chiricahua National Monument (Hwy 181 to E Bonita Canyon Rd, Willcox) - Grab a park map and hike through the volcanic pinnacles that define Chiricahua National Monument. I recommend the moderate one-way hike (mostly downhill) starting from Massai Point and back to the Visitor Center (7.5 miles). Take the convenient hiker's shuttle, which leaves from the Visitor Center at 8:30 am. Personal vehicles can be driven to all overlooks along the scenic eight-mile Bonita Canyon Drive. For those with less time, hike the Echo Canyon Loop trail through "The Grottoes". For an easy stroll, the .25-mile interpretive trail through the Faraway Historic Ranch District offers interesting interpretation of the historic buildings. Free.

NEW MEXICO

Alamogordo   Carlsbad

ALAMOGORDO

5 hours from Chiricahua National Monument, AZ

Vacationing in style, White Sands National Monument

Note: Alamogordo is the starting point for many interesting attractions in southern New Mexico, most notably White Sands National Monument. Explore the many natural, historical, and cultural sites, as well as excellent camping opportunities. Alamogordo is two hours from Roswell, NM (famous for the 1947 UFO incident), however, Roswell's UFO museum is sorely outdated and not worth the diversion—unless you are a die-hard UFO fanatic!

CAMPING

Oliver Lee Memorial State Park (Hwy 54, 15 miles south of Alamogordo) – This desert park offers a campground with 44 developed sites (18 full RV hookups). Restrooms, showers, and dump station on-site. Interpretive trails meander along lush Dog Creek, and guided tours are offered at Oliver Lee's restored ranch house (a setting for Hollywood films). Fees: Tent $10, RV (35' max length) $14-$18. Most sites are first come, first served, but reservations can be made for a handful of sites at www.new-mexicostateparks.reserveamerica.com. Park phone: (575) 437-8284

Three Rivers Petroglyph Site BLM Campground (455 3 Rivers Road, Tularosa, 35 miles north of Alamogordo) – This small, first-come campground is located at the renowned Three Rivers Petroglyph Site, which offers an interpretive trail to view ancient Mogollon rock art. There are 12 campsites and two full RV hookups. Water, BBQ grills, and vault toilets on-site. Fees: Tent $7, RV with hookups (30' max length) $18. BLM District phone: (575) 525-4300.

James Canyon Forest Service Campground (35 miles east of Alamogordo, along US Hwy 82 in Mayhill, NM) – This first-come, first-served campground (open April-Nov) is located at 6,800 ft within the scenic Lincoln National Forest. Seven campsites available (two sites are drive up—all others require a short walk across a small bridge). Vault toilet on-site. RV max length 16' (no hookups). Free. District phone: (575) 257-4095.

MUST-SEE ATTRACTIONS

White Sands National Monument (Hwy 70, Alamogordo) – White Sands National Monument encompasses the largest glistening gypsum sand dune fields in the world. A must-see if you're driving through southern New Mexico. Park rangers offer short interpretive hikes and longer, more strenuous hikes through the dunes. Fees: Park entry $5 per person. No camping allowed in the park.

New Mexico Museum of Space History (5004 Hwy 2001, Alamogordo) – For the traveling space enthusiast, the Museum of Space History exhibits real space artifacts, full sized replicas of rockets, a mock-up of the International Space Station, and the burial site of Ham—the first chimpanzee launched into space. The museum also offers an IMAX Theater and planetarium for an additional fee. Outdoor exhibits are free. Admission: Adults $8-$16, Child (age 4-12) $6-$11, Children 3 and under (Free).

Oliver Lee Memorial State Park (Hwy 54, 15 miles south of Alamogordo) – Set against the backdrop of the Sacramento Mountains, this State Park features unique interpretive trails that meander along lush Dog Creek deep into Dog Creek Canyon. Guided tours are offered at Oliver Lee's historic 19th-century restored ranch house (a setting for Hollywood films). Camping available. Day use fee: $5

Three Rivers Petroglyph Site, New Mexico

CARLSBAD

3 hours from Alamogordo, NM

Cave entrance and amphitheater for bat exodus, Carlsbad Caverns

Note: Carlsbad is the launching point for the Carlsbad Caverns—a spectacular, must-see destination on this travel itinerary.

CAMPING

Brantley Lake State Park Campground (33 East Brantley Lake Road, Carlsbad) – This State Park campground offers 51 developed tent and RV sites, with tent sites on the lakefront. Full RV hookups, water, restrooms and showers on-site. Recreation includes hiking, boating, swimming, and fishing. Fees: Tent $10, RV (35' max length) $14. Park phone: (575) 457-2384. Reservations can be made at www.newmexicostateparks.reserveamerica.com.

Guadalupe Mountains National Park Pine Springs Campground (Hwy 180 in Salt Flat, TX, two hours SE of Carlsbad) – This first-come, first-served campground is located within Guadalupe Mountains National Park, just over the NM border in Texas. The campground offers 19 RV sites (no hookups) and 20 tent sites. Drinking water and developed restrooms on-site. There is a Visitor Center and museum, as well as excellent hiking throughout the park. Fees: Tent and RV (55' max length) $8. Park phone: (915) 828-3251

Avalon Reservoir (three miles north of Carlsbad, from Hwy 285 turn left on Canal Street, go three miles, turn left on Avalon Road) – This Department of Fish and Game area offers primitive RV and tent camping along the reservoir. Swimming and fishing allowed year-around. Note: The road along the reservoir is unpaved. Free.

MUST-SEE ATTRACTIONS

Carlsbad Caverns National Park (Hwy 62/180 at Whites City, NM) – Carlsbad Caverns National Park is a system of 117 caves open for self-guided exploration and ranger-led tours. The park offers a 1.5-mile, self-guided cave tour through the natural entrance to Carlsbad Cavern, or starting at the lower cave via the underground elevator. In summer, watch the incredible exodus of Mexican free-tail bats out of the cavern at dusk (see park schedule). Fees: Park entry $10; Ranger-led tours $7-$20. No camping available.

Guadalupe Mountains National Park (Hwy 180 in Salt Flat, TX, two hours SE of Carlsbad) – When heading back to I-10, consider visiting Guadalupe Mountains National Park, just over the NM border in the West Texas panhandle. There is a visitor center and museum, as well as excellent hiking opportunities. Ascend the difficult Guadalupe Peak Trail to the highest peak in Texas, or hike the easy-moderate McKittrick Canyon Trail lined with Bigtooth maples and a meandering stream. Late fall and winter are the best times to visit. Camping available.

Pecos National Historical Park (1 Peach Drive, Pecos) – If taking Hwy 285 south to I-10 (from Carlsbad), don't miss this wonderful historical park. It offers visitors a peak into the confluence of New Mexico's cultural and Civil War history, with its on-site ancestral pueblo, an historic Spanish mission, and a Civil War hiking trail which tells the story of the Battle of Glorieta Pass. The Visitor Center features an excellent museum with historic artifacts, and walking or jeep tours are offered daily. Free admission.

Pecos National Historical Park, New Mexico

TEXAS

Sonora   San Antonio   New Braunfels   Austin   Houston

Note: Driving through a state as big as Texas can be daunting. West Texas is an open, desert landscape; east Texas is green and mountainous. There are unique camping and recreational opportunities along the entire route. Highway rest stops are a great, free overnight resource in Texas. They are clean and many have free Wifi! Check your atlas for various locations along the route.

SONORA
5 hours from Carlsbad Caverns, NM

Crystal Cave, Caverns of Sonora

Note: Sonora is famous for its marvelous "living" calcite caverns at the privately-owned Caverns of Sonora (with a convenient campground on-site). This stop is not to be missed, if just for one night.

CAMPING

Caverns of Sonora RV Park and Tent Campground (Exit 392 from I-10, turn south on Caverns of Sonora Road, follow signs to the private road leading to the park) – This 48-site campground is located on a quiet working ranch (with resident peacocks) on the Caverns of Sonora property. Full hookups, bathrooms with free showers, and gift shop offering homemade fudge on-site. Fees: Tent and RV (40' max length) $15-$25. Call (325) 387-3105 for reservations.

TX I-10 Rest Area at Mile Marker 394 (Sonora, TX) – Highway rest stop with running water, bathrooms, and picnic tables. Free.

MUST-SEE ATTRACTIONS

Caverns of Sonora (Exit 392 from I-10, take Caverns of Sonora Road, and follow signs to the private road leading into the park) – This living, growing cave system is one of the best in Texas, and its private owners go to great lengths to protect it. Its unrivaled beauty is not to be missed. The Crystal Palace Tour is approximately 1.75 hours and two miles in length (easy to moderate); or try the 4-hour rappelling tour into the Devil's Pit. Admission: Adults $20, Child (age 4-11) $16, Children under 4 Free. Tickets can be reserved online at www.cavernsofsonora. com. Phone: (325) 387-3105.

SAN ANTONIO

2.5 hours from Sonora, TX

Note: San Antonio is a beautiful and historic city, and many of its attractions are free. Just west of San Antonio, take a quick 5-mile detour to Ingram, TX and visit Stonehenge II. It offers a replica of England's original stone monument, as well as replicas of the massive Easter Island carved heads or "moai" (120 Point Theatre Road S, Ingram, TX).

Riverwalk cafe and boat canal, San Antonio

CAMPING

Government Canyon State Natural Area (12861 Galm Road, San Antonio) – A tent camper's paradise (sorry, no RVs), Government Canyon offers 40 miles of nature and wilderness trails with preserved dinosaur tracks, an historic ranch house, and a plethora of wildlife. The campground offers 23 walk-in sites (50 yards from the parking lot). Drinking water, bathrooms, BBQ grills and food storage lockers on-site. Fees: Park entry $7, Tent camping $18. Reservations can be made online at www.texasreserveworld.com.

San Antonio KOA (602 Gembler Road, San Antonio) – This highly rated, full-service KOA campground is noted for its cleanliness, friendly staff, and spacious, shady campsites (cabins are also available). Recreation includes scenic multi-use trails, pedal cart rentals, a heated pool, and playground. Breakfast and hot pizza available for purchase. Fees: Tent $35-$45, RV (90' max length) $40-$80, Cabins $70-$140. Reservations can be made by calling (210) 224-9296 or online at www.koa.com/camp-grounds/san-antonio/.

Alamo River RV Ranch and Campground (12430 Trawalter Lane, Von Ormy) – Located 16 miles south of downtown San Antonio, Alamo River is a pleasant RV and tent camping park situated along the Medina river in oak woodland habitat. Full RV hookups, secluded tent camping sites, and a private rental cottage available. Showers, laundry, and free Wifi on-site. Fees: Tent $25-$30, RV (70' max length) $44-$48, Private cottage $65-$150. Reservations can be made by phone at (210) 622-5022 or online at www.alamoriver. com.

Guadalupe County Safety Rest Area (I-10 at milepost 621, east of Senguin, TX) – This is an excellent rest area if you are leaving San Antonio and need a quick overnight stop (approximately 37 miles east of downtown San Antonio). Renovated in 2006 with new restrooms, nature trail and playground. Free.

MUST-SEE ATTRACTIONS

San Antonio River Walk (downtown San Antonio) – Hailed as the number one tourist attraction in Texas, the river walk is a network of winding walkways along the banks of the San Antonio River. Lined by shops and riverside cafés, it is also the jumping-off point to major tourist attractions and historic sites. Parking available at Rivercenter Mall (849 E Commerce Street) and throughout downtown San Antonio.

The Alamo (300 Alamo Plaza, located just off the Riverwalk) – Originally serving as the Mission San Antonio de Valero, this site was occupied as a military station throughout the 1800s by the Spanish, Rebels, and Mexicans, ultimately playing a critical role in the Texas Revolution. Self-guided tours and docents on-site. Free.

Mission San José (6710 San Jose Drive, San Antonio) – The most spectacular mission on San Antonio's Mission Trail, Mission San José is famous for its imposing architecture and Mariachi masses on Sunday. The Mission houses a Visitor Center, which provides a 20-minute introductory video (recommended), a working grain mill, and free guided walking tours every hour. Free.

Brackenridge Park (3853 N. Saint Mary's Street, San Antonio) – A 343-acre park with a lush Japanese tea garden as its main attraction. The garden is lined with numerous pathways, koi ponds and a striking pagoda. The park also houses the 35-acre San Antonio Zoo. Admission: Japanese Tea Garden (Free); Zoo: Adult $16.50, Child (age 3-11) $13.25, Children ages 3 and under (Free).

San Antonio Museum of Art (200 West Jones Avenue, located just off the Riverwalk) – Located in the historic Lone Star Brewery building in downtown San Antonio, this beautiful museum houses diverse collections from around the world, rotating exhibitions, and an award-winning cafe. Admission: Adult $15, Children under 12 (Free). Admission is free to visitors Tues 4-9 p.m. and Sun 10am-12pm.

AUSTIN
1.25 hours from San Antonio

Boating scenic Lady Bird Lake, Austin

Note: Austin is a bit of a diversion (up I-35), however, an essential destination for those interested in its eclectic music and people scene, its numerous city festivals, and its unique juxtaposition as the "liberal" capital of Texas. In addition, there are great tubing and kayaking opportunities along the Guadalupe/Comal Rivers in New Braunfels (see below).

CAMPING

McKinney Falls State Park (5808 McKinney Falls Parkway, 13 miles SE of Austin) – This hill country park offers miles of winding trails, excellent for biking and walking; as well as fishing and swimming along Onion Creek. There are 69 tent and RV sites with full hookups. Restrooms, showers, and fire rings with grills on-site. Fees: Day use fee $6, Tent $15, RV (50' max length) $20-$24. Reservations can be made by phone at (512) 389-8900 or online at www.texas.reserveworld.com.

Windy Point Park (6506 Bob Wentz Park Road/Comanche Trail—follow signs to Windy Point Park) – Located 19 miles NW of Austin, this first-come, first-served county park campground is situated on the shores of picturesque Lake Travis. It offers shade trees on a natural grass lawn and recreational opportunities like boating and scuba diving (deep water access only, take caution if swimming). Suitable for tent and full-sized RV camping (no hookups). No pets allowed. Drinking water, bathrooms and hot showers available. Fees: Day use fee $8, Tent and RV $10 (6pm to 10am). Park phone: (512) 266-3337.

MUST-SEE ATTRACTIONS

Guadalupe/Comal River Tubing (New Braunfels) – New Braunfels (situated between San Antonio and Austin off I-35) is the lazy river float capital of south Texas, and home to numerous tubing outfitters. Packages include tube/kayak rentals and transportation up the Guadalupe/Comal rivers, with floats ranging from one to four hours in length. The float season is typically spring through summer depending on river flow. Call Whitewater Sports in New Braunfels at (830) 964-3800 for river updates. Rentals: $24 per person. Coupon for $5 off at www.floattheguadalupe.com.

Texas State Capitol Building (112 East 11th Street, Austin) – The Renaissance Revival-style Capitol building is recognized as one of the nation's largest and most distinguished. Self-guided tours of the grounds and Capitol building are available. I recommend the free 45-minute guided tours led by knowledgeable in-house volunteers. Free.

South Congress Street Walking Tour (tour starts at the south entrance of the Capitol building) – Take a stroll through Austin's 19th century historic district. The Congress Avenue & Sixth Street Tour includes historic commerce buildings, hotels, and cathedrals. Tour times are 9am Tuesday, Thursday, Friday, and Saturday, and 11am and 1pm on Sunday. Advanced reservations highly recommended. Call the Austin Visitor Center at (512) 478-0098 or reserve online at www.austintexas.org. Free.

Congress Avenue Bridge Bats (220 South Congress Avenue) – Approximately 1.5 million bats emerge nightly from under the Congress Avenue Bridge from March through August. Excellent vantage points for viewing bats include the Statesman Bat Observation Center or any sidewalk (or waterfront café) on the south end of the bridge. Boat rental outfits along the waterfront offer bat tours as well. Call the Bat Hotline at (512) 416-5700 (ext 3636) to get daily updates on when the bats emerge.

6th Street (7 blocks between I-35 and Congress Avenue) – 6th Street is the heart of Austin's live entertainment scene. Much of 6th street is for the younger, late-night crowd, with its numerous bars and funky cafes. For the less rowdy crowd, I recommend the elegant and historic Driskill Hotel for a happy hour cocktail.

Capitol Building, Austin

HOUSTON

2.5 hrs. from Austin

City park and skyline, Houston

Note: Houston is an overnight stop, not a must-see destination on this itinerary—unless you are itching to visit it! There are a few attractions that warrant mentioning, as well as excellent State Park camping in the vicinity.

CAMPING

Brazos Bend State Park (21901 FM 762, Needville) – Located approximately one hour south of downtown Houston, this lush park is situated on 5,000 acres of lakes, with live oak trees draped in Spanish moss. Tent and large RV camping with full hookups, restrooms with showers, and BBQ grills on-site. Screened shelters (with water and electricity) are also available. Fees: Park entry (age 13-adult) $7, Tent $12, RV (no length limit) $20-$25; Screened shelter $25. Reservations can be made by phone at (512) 389-8900 or online at www.texas.reserveworld.com.

Double Lake Campground (301 FM 2025, Coldspring) – Located approximately one hour north of Houston (within the Sam Houston National Forest), this campground features a swim and boat-friendly lake with sites abutting the forest. Wildlife sightings are almost guaranteed. Full RV hookups, pull-thru and tent sites available; showers, dump station, and general store on-site. Rates: Day use fee $7, Tent $20, RV (no length limit) $20-$40.

MUST-SEE ATTRACTIONS

Space Center Houston at Johnson Space Center (1601 NASA Pkwy, Houston) – Located 20 miles SE of Houston, NASA's Johnson Space Center is the home of astronaut training and Mission Control, and the only place in the world where visitors can watch astronauts train for missions. Take a behind-the-scenes tram tour or visit the space museum. Admission: Adults $29.95, Child (age 4-11) $24.95, Children age 3 and under (Free); Level 9 Tram Tour: $125.00 (limited seating, advanced reservations recommended at www www.spacecenter.org).

San Jacinto Battleground State Historic Site (3523 Independence Parkway South, LaPorte) – Located 30 minutes east of downtown Houston, this National Historic Landmark consists of a self-guided walking tour of the famous San Jacinto Battleground, where Santa Ana's forces were defeated. Visit its 489-foot monument and observation tower (with elevator); the history museum; and the Battleship Texas, the only surviving relic naval vessel which served in both World Wars. Admission: Monument and Museum (Free); Battleship Tour and Exhibitions: Adult $16.50, Child (age 0-11) $12.50.

Hermann Park (6100 Hermann Park Drive, Houston) – Located in the heart of Houston, Hermann Park's 445 acres is home to various botanical and sculpture gardens, nature trails, a pioneer log house museum, the Hermann Park Railroad, and the Houston Zoo. Pedal boating around McGovern Lake is a popular pastime, followed by lunch at the park's Pinewood Café. Admission: Gardens (Free); Zoo: Adult $18, Child (age 2-11) $14; Pedal boats: $11 per boat; Train: $3.50 per person.

Brazos Bend State Park (21901 FM 762, Needville) – Located approximately one hour south of downtown Houston, Brazos Bend features mystical, moss-draped oak and hardwood forests situated on 5,000 acres of wetland lakes, marshes, and swamps. It is also home to a good-sized population of alligators. Various boardwalks and paved foot trails allow you to explore the park by foot or bike. The George Observatory is also located within the park and is open to visitors on Saturdays from 3pm-10pm.

Hermann Park, Houston

LOUISIANA

New Orleans

NEW ORLEANS
5 hrs. from Houston, TX

Jackson Square, New Orleans

Note: New Orleans is notably a must-see destination on this itinerary. Many of its popular French Quarter attractions can be tourist traps (e.g., French Market, Bourbon Street), so don't miss the alternatives listed here. State Park campgrounds also offer unique recreational opportunities in bayou and plantation country (listed below).

CAMPING

Bayou Segnette State Park (7777 Westbank Expressway, Westwego) – Located approximately 12 miles south of New Orleans across the Mississippi River, this State Park offers 98 tent and large RV sites with full hookups in an open, grassy environment. Recreation includes boating, fishing and swimming, nature trails, and a children's playground with wave pool. Take the free ferry from Algiers (6.5 miles from the park) to downtown New Orleans. It is a great alternative to expensive parking in the French Quarter. Fees: Park entry $3, Tent and RV $25-$33. Park phone: (888) 677-2296. Reservations can be made online at www.reserveamerica.com.

Fairview Riverside State Park (119 Fairview Drive, Madisonville) – Located approximately 38 miles north of New Orleans, this 81-site, full-service campground is situated on the shores of Lake Ponchartrain and bounds the lovely Tchefuncte River. Water recreation can be enjoyed on both the river and lake. The Otis House Museum—a National Historic Landmark—fronts the lake and is available for tours. Fees: Tent and RV (no length limit) $14-$28; Otis House Museum: Adults and Children $4, Children under age 3 and seniors (Free). Park phone: (888) 677-3247. Reservations can be made online at www. reserveamerica.com.

Jude Travel Park (7400 Chef Menteur Hwy, New Orleans) – This full-service RV park (55' max length) is located 5 miles from the French Quarter. It is quite urban, but amenities are clean and the sites are situated among shade trees and a grassy lawn. The park offers a shuttle to the French Quarter (limited hours). Wifi, showers and laundry on-site. Fees: Tent and RV (up to 29') $30. Call (504) 241-0632 for reservations (and rates for RVs over 29').

St. Bernard State Park (501 St. Bernard Parkway, Braithwaite) – This family-friendly park is located 16 miles SE of New Orleans along the banks of the Mississippi. It offers 51 tent and RV sites with full hookups. Recreation includes a network of man-made lagoons to explore, a wetland nature trail, and a children's water play area. Restrooms, showers, BBQ grills, and swimming pool on-site. Fees: Tent and RV (no length limit) $20-$28. Park phone: (888) 677-7823. Reservations can be made online at www.reserveamerica.com.

I-10 Rest Area at Exit #2 (just across the eastern border in Westonia, MS) – This rest stop is located 51 miles east of New Orleans near the Stennis Space Center (a convenient stop if you are leaving the city in the evening). It offers separate parking for RVs and 18-wheelers along the on-ramp and can be a bit noisy. Dump station and water available. Free.

MUST-SEE ATTRACTIONS

Note: Parking in the French Quarter (FQ) is almost impossible, but there are many parking garages within five blocks of the FQ if you are willing and able to walk the distance. (The walk is quite interesting and lovely.) Iberville Street has many garages to choose from, and RV friendly parking is available (before noon) in the open lots next to Jax Brewery (600 Decatur Street).

French Quarter Visitor Center (419 Decatur Street) – The Visitor Center is a great starting point to get yourself oriented to the French Quarter and its attractions. Located two blocks east of Jackson Square, it provides city maps, tour information, and knowledgeable staff to answer your questions.

Free Tours by Foot-French Quarter (meets at the Andrew Jackson statue in Jackson Square) – I highly recommend this two-hour, free walking tour. Well-versed guides narrate New Orleans history, walking at a leisurely pace (one mile) to hidden gems throughout the FQ. Reservations are required due to this tour's popularity (they will turn you away at the meeting spot without one). Tips are greatly appreciated. Tours (walking and bike) are offered at 10am and 2pm. For reservations call (504) 222-2967 or book online at www.freetoursbyfoot.com.

St. Louis Cathedral (located on Jackson Square) – A National Historic Landmark, St. Louis Cathedral is open and free to the public (except during mass services). Behind the Cathedral lies the Old Ursuline Convent (1100 Chartes Street), the oldest building in the Mississippi Valley. Daily self-guided tours of the convent are available from 10am to 4pm.

Frenchmen Street – Down river from the French Quarter (at the far end of French Market) is the Faubourg Marigny neighborhood and its famed Frenchman Street. A legendary hub of music and nightlife, you'll enjoy numerous outdoor musicians and unique music venues. It is best to go in the evening, but do not stray off the main thoroughfare at night (and no further than the Faubourg Marigny neighborhood) due to thievery in the area.

Café du Monde (500 Port of New Orleans) – This coffee and beignet (French donut) shop is a famous landmark in the French Quarter. The Jackson Square location (800 Decatur Street) is very crowded, with waits up to one hour. The lesser-known Port of New Orleans location (listed here) is much less crowded, and the beignets are just as tasty. It is located inside The Outlet Collection at Riverwalk mall (one mile from Jackson Square) and provides quaint outdoor seating along the edge of the Mississippi River.

French Quarter Restaurants – The FQ is famous for its oyster bars and Cajun fare. The following restaurants are highly recommended for the traveling foodie: Mulate's Cajun (210 Julia St), Court of Two Sisters (613 Royal St— or just peek inside the beautiful garden patio), Bourbon Oyster House (144 Bourbon St), Casamento's Restaurant and Oyster House (4330 Magazine St—this restaurant is located away from the hubbub of the FQ).

Oak Alley, New Orleans

Visit Plantations on the Great Mississippi River Road – Louisiana's River Road (State Hwy 18) consists of a 70-mile corridor along the Mississippi River between New Orleans and Baton Rouge. I recommend visiting the following plantations (while traveling NW along Hwy 18): Evergreen Plantation (includes the original complex buildings and slave quarters—4677 State Hwy 18, Edgard); the Laura Plantation (Creole plantation in the Federal architectural style—2247 State Hwy 18, Vacherie); Oak Alley Plantation (Greek Revival architecture—3645 State Hwy 18, Vacherie); and the San Francisco Plantation House (the most ornate of the plantation houses—2646 Hwy 44, Garyville, cross the river at Wallace).

Honey Island Swamp Tours (41490 Crawford Landing Road, Slidell) – For a little taste of the Louisiana bayou, this two-hour tour is a fun diversion within the 250-square mile Honey Island Swamp. Expect to see alligators, herons, egrets, turtles, and some rascally raccoons; as well as interesting historic river homes and fishing shacks. Call (985) 641-1769 for reservations. Tour: Adult $23, Child $15.

FLORIDA

Pensacola | Crystal River/ Homosassa Springs | St Petersburg/ Sarasota | Fort Meyers Beach | The Everglades | The Keys

Note: The drive through southern Mississippi and Alabama is short, so we are continuing to Florida, the Sunshine State, with its plethora of must-see attractions. These include pristine shelling beaches, hot springs, wildlife preserves, historic sites, and barrier island snorkeling, to name a few. Our focus is on western Florida, the Everglades, and the Keys.

PENSACOLA
3 hours from New Orleans, LA

Johnson Beach, Perdido Key

Note: Pensacola's white sand beaches make for a beautiful, overnight stop-over when entering the Sunshine

State. The town offers restaurants and grocery stores, but the real draw is the National Seashore. Closures are possible during hurricane season.

CAMPING

Gulf Islands National Seashore—Fort Pickens Campground (1400 Fort Pickens Road) – This 180-site tent and RV campground is located on a pristine barrier island between the Gulf of Mexico and Pensacola Bay. Campsites are within ¼ mile of the beach, and historic Fort Pickens is one mile away. Full hookups, dump station, restrooms with showers, and camp store on-site. Fees: Tent and RV (50' max length) $26. Park phone for updates on closures (850) 934-2622. Reservations can be made online at www.recreation.gov.

MUST-SEE ATTRACTIONS

Johnson Beach National Seashore (Johnson Beach Road, Pensacola) – Johnson Beach is an unspoiled, white sand beach on Pensacola's famous Perdido Key. This narrow key offers gulf and bay views, and features a half-mile Discovery Trail. This raised boardwalk takes you through dunes, pine trees, salt marsh outlooks, and brings you to a beautiful view of Grand Lagoon. You'll likely see many shorebirds and marine life during your visit. Admission (per car): $20 (good for 7 days at all Gulf Island National Seashore locations)

Peg Leg Pete's Oyster Bar (1010 Fort Pickens Road) – This family-friendly waterfront cafe at Pensacola Beach has an award-winning atmosphere, great food at low prices, and offers live music on the weekends. There is a gift shop on-site for fun Florida souvenirs and t-shirts.

ST. JOSEPH PENINSULA

3.5 hours from Pensacola

T.H. Stone Memorial St. Joseph Peninsula State Park, Port St. Joe

Note: St. Joseph Peninsula is an excellent camping stopover between Panama City and Tallahassee, along the Gulf Coast's U.S. 98. It is a hidden gem I'd recommend visiting more than one night—its beaches, clear waters, and sand dunes are stunning.

CAMPING

T.H. Stone Memorial St. Joseph Peninsula State Park (8899 Cape San Blas Road, Port St. Joe) – This beautiful and remote park is situated along a 10-mile stretch of white sandy beach along the Gulf Coast, with some of the tallest sand dunes in the state. The clear water of St. Joseph Bay is great for boating, kayaking, and fishing; and the four-mile paved path through the park is great for biking. The campground offers 119 RV and tent sites (as well as cabins with kitchens, bathrooms, heat and air) just steps from the Gulf. Full hookups, dump station, BBQ grills, restrooms and showers on-site. Fees: Tent and RV (40' max length) $24, Cabins $100.

TRENTON

4 hours from St Joseph Peninsula

Peaceful Suwannee River, Florida

Note: You are probably wondering—Trenton? Besides being a convenient four hour stop past Port St. Joe, Trenton holds some of my favorite Florida memories. Otter Springs Park and Campground is a hidden gem for water recreation along the Suwannee River (the inspiration for the minstrel song "Old Folks at Home" and now the Florida state song).

CAMPING

Otter Springs Park and Campground (6470 SW 80th Avenue, Trenton) – This private RV and tent campground has a gorgeous hot spring on-site which flows into the Suwannee River. Recreation includes swimming and canoeing, hiking, biking and birding. There is a heated Olympic-sized swimming pool (housed within a screened-in pavilion) on-site. Full hookups, BBQ grills, showers and laundry available. There are also three cabins and an historic stilt house (with all amenities) available for overnight stays. Fees: Park entry $3, Tent $24, RV $31, Cabin $82-$93, Stilt House $115.

Manatee Springs State Park (11650 N.W. 115th Street, Chiefland) – This full-service campground and park is located just south of Trenton and is a good alternative to Otter Springs. Manatee Springs is popular for swimming, boating, snorkeling, and cave diving (rentals available). Amenities include full hookups, dump station, BBQ grills, playground, bathrooms and showers. Fees: Park entry $6, Tent and RV (35' max length) $20.

MUST-SEE ATTRACTIONS

Otter Springs Canoeing (Otter Springs Park and Campground—see Camping) – Otter Springs feeds into the Suwannee River a ½ mile from its origin at the park. The crystal-clear spring and its abundance of wildlife (otter, deer, herons, and cranes) make for excellent photo opportunities. Paddling up the slow-moving Suwannee River is fairly easy, and an interesting contrast to the clear spring. Consider paddling downriver to nearby Fanning Springs (6.8 miles) for a complete adventure. Canoe rentals available at the Otter Springs campground store.

Manatee Springs Canoeing and Hiking (Manatee Springs State Park—see Camping) – Walk along the boardwalk, swim, snorkel, scuba dive, or canoe the crystal-clear spring (rentals available at the concession stand). The spring meanders through a mystical cypress forest about 1/4 mile to the Suwannee, and in winter manatees swim upstream to the spring's headwaters. You will spot numerous white-tailed deer and water birds here as well.

CRYSTAL RIVER AND HOMOSASSA SPRINGS

1.25 hours from Trenton

Three Sisters Spring, Homosassa

Note: Crystal River and Homosassa Springs are a short drive from Trenton—and within a 15-minute drive from one another. Crystal springs and Florida wildlife are abundant here, and I would recommend at least a two-night stay in this quintessential Florida locale.

CAMPING

Chassahowitzka River Campground (8600 W. Miss Maggie Drive, Homosassa) – This private campground offers 53 full-service RV sites, 28 primitive tent sites, boat ramps, general store, laundry facilities, and kayak rentals. The campground sits along the Chassahowitzka River, dotted with crystal springs and an abundance of wildlife—including manatee and the elusive river dolphin. Fees: Tent $23, RV (50' max length) $38. Reservations can be made by calling (352) 382-2200 (preferred) or by email at chascamp@tampabay.rr.com.

Rock Crusher Canyon RV Park (237 S. Rock Crusher Road, Crystal River) – This spacious RV park is serene and wooded, and ideally situated near all must-see attractions in Homosassa. It offers full hookups, free cable and Wifi, screened pool and spa. Fees: RV (80' max length) $35–$45. No tent camping available.

Crystal Isles RV Resort (11419 W. Fort Island Trail, Crystal River) – This full-service RV resort is situated on the King's Bay canal system with large, grassy camp-sites. Tent sites, camping trailers, and cottages also available. Amenities include Wifi, heated pool, showers, laundry, golf and tennis courts. Fees: Tent $32, RV (80' max length) $36–$60, Cottage rental $75–$95. Call (877) 570-2267 for reservations or visit www.rvonthego.com/florida/crystal-isles-rv-resort/

Silver Lake Campground-Withlacoochee State Forest (31475 Silver Lake Road, Brooksville) – Located about 30 mins. SE of Homosassa Springs, this RV and tent campground offers 23 campsites, all on the lakeshore, nestled under an open shade of oaks. The park offers a canoe and boat launch, nature trails and boardwalk. Amenities include full hookups, restrooms, showers and dump station. All sites are self-register. Fees: RV sites with full hookups (55' max length) $20-$24, Non-electric sites with water $15, Primitive sites $10. Note: There are two other campgrounds within this recreational complex (Cypress Glen—34 campsites with electricity; and Crooked River—tent camping only).

Resident manatee, Homosassa Springs Wildlife State Park

MUST-SEE ATTRACTIONS

Ellie Schiller Homosassa Springs Wildlife State Park (4150 S. Suncoast Blvd, Homosassa) – This renowned State Park offers some of the best wildlife viewing in the state. The park offers a Visitor Center and a ranger-narrated boat ride up the springs to the Wildlife Park. The park offers an underwater observatory for viewing manatee year-around, an exceptional aviary, and a boardwalk for viewing alligators, wildcats, and black bear. I recommend walking the easy, one-mile trail back to the Visitor Center. Fees: Adult (age 13 and over) $13, Child (age 6-12) $5, Children 5 and under (Free).

Three Sisters Springs (Crystal River National Wildlife Refuge, 267 N.W. Third St, Crystal River) – Three Sisters Springs is accessible by kayak up Crystal River into the Three Springs area. The springs can get crowded with boaters and locals, however, possible manatee sightings make it a worthwhile endeavor. If you have snorkel gear bring it along for underwater viewing. Kayaks can be rented from Manatee Tour and Dive at the address listed above. Fees: Kayak rental $25-$65.

Crystal River Preserve State Park (3266 N Sailboat Ave)/ **Crystal River Archaeological State Park** (3400 N. Museum Point) – These two State Parks are managed side-by-side and offer unique recreational opportunities distinctive to Crystal River. The Preserve offers interpretive trails, eco-boat tours, sunset cruises, and kayak rentals. The Archaeological Park is a 61-acre National Historic Landmark featuring numerous Native American burial and temple mounds, as well as a sizable midden site. Admission: Free. Parking at the Archaeological State Park is $3.

Cracker's Bar and Grill (502 NW 6th St, Crystal River) – This beautiful waterfront restaurant is a great family-friendly stop for lunch or dinner after a day of fun. The large outdoor patio offers an excellent view overlooking Crystal River. Their specialties include grouper sandwiches and conch fritters (a regional favorite). The food is abundant and reasonably priced.

ST. PETERSBURG AND SARASOTA

1.5 hours from Homosassa Springs

Weedon Island State Preserve from the observation tower, St Petersburg

Kim's Travel Guide for RV and Tent Camping in the USA

Note: St. Petersburg and Sarasota are within a one-hour drive of each other. Each offer must-see city attractions and recreational opportunities. I recommend at least two days of exploring here.

CAMPING

Fort De Soto Park Campground (3500 Pinellas Bayway S, Tierra Verde) – Fort De Soto County Park is made up of five interconnected islands (keys) near St. Petersburg, all offering a surplus of wildlife and recreational opportunities. The campground offers 238 full-service RV and tent sites. Wifi, camp store, and laundry facilities on-site. Recreation includes multipurpose trails, canoe/kayak rentals, shelling, and a children's play area. Be advised, there are numerous toll bridges to get here, but it's well worth the inconvenience. Rates: Tent and RV (no length limit) $30-$40. Advanced reservations are recommended and best made by calling (727) 582-2267.

Myakka River State Park (13208 State Road 72, Sarasota) – The beautiful Myakka Wild and Scenic River flows for 14 miles through this State Park. The park offers three campgrounds with full hookups, restrooms and hot showers. Fees: Park entry $6, Tent and RV (35' max length) $26, Log cabin rental $70. Book online at www.reserveamerica.com or call (800) 326-3521.

Oscar Scherer State Park (Six miles south of Sarasota, 1843 S. Tamiami Trail, Osprey) – This park lies on pristine Lake Osprey, offering recreational opportunities such as snorkeling, canoeing and hiking. There are 94 RV and tent sites, full hookups, hot showers and laundry facilities. Fees: Tent and RV (36' max length) $26. Book online at www.reserveamerica.com or call (800) 326-3521.

MUST-SEE ATTRACTIONS

Weedon Island State Preserve (1800 Weedon Drive NE, St. Petersburg) – Weedon Island State Preserve offers some of the best mangrove kayaking and cultural history in the Old Tampa Bay area. The park offers a Cultural and Natural History Center (free admission), extensive board-walk trails, observation tower, and marked kayak trails through the mangrove tunnels (highly recommended!) Wildlife often spotted include armadillo, turtles, dolphins, and water birds. Kayak rentals available on-site ($17-$50 hourly).

Siesta Key (6 miles south of Sarasota off I-41. Turn right onto Siesta Drive and travel approximately four miles to Siesta Village) – Siesta Key is an eight-mile long barrier island famous for having the "world's whitest beaches". The sparkling and serene Gulf of Mexico lies to the west, and Sarasota Bay and Florida's Intracoastal Waterway lie to the east. Snorkel at the famous Point of Rocks (west end) or spend an afternoon in Siesta Village shopping and dining.

John and Mabel Ringling Museum of Art (5401 Bay Shore Road, Sarasota) – This fabulous gulf shore mansion and museum was home to John Ringling, one of the five original circus kings of the Ringling Brothers and Barnum & Bailey Circus. It includes tours of the Venetian Goth-ic mansion Cà d'Zan, the Circus Museum, the 21-gallery Art Museum which houses many great Old Masters, and the beautiful Bayfront Gardens. Tours are self-guided or led by a docent throughout the day. Admission: Adult $25, Child (age 6-17) $5. Discount Thursdays (5pm-8pm): Adult $15, Child $5.

Sarasota Classic Car Museum (5500 N. Tamiami Trail, Sarasota) – Located across the street from the Ringling Museum, this museum features an exceptional history of the automobile from the horseless carriage to one-of-a kind European and exotic classics. Some notable exhibits include the original Batmobile, John and Mable Ringling's collection of Rolls Royce autos, and John Lennon's 1965 Mercedes Benz. Admission: Adult $12.85, Child (age 6-12) $7.25, Children 5 years and under (Free).

Myakka River State Park (13208 State Road 72, Sarasota) – Located along the beautiful Myakka Wild and Scenic River, the park features scenic airboat tours as well as canoe and kayak rentals. There are a number of hiking trails and a 74-ft tower to view the wetlands from above. Please note, it can get quite flooded in the summer months.

Oscar Scherer State Park (Six miles south of Sarasota, 1843 S. Tamiami Trail, Osprey) – This park lies on both Lake Osprey (great for swimming and snorkeling) and South Creek (great for canoeing and kayaking). Ranger-led canoe tours are offered on Wednesdays, and canoe/ kayak rentals available daily. The park also offers six nature trails and an Interpretive Nature Center.

Aerial view of Siesta Key, Sarasota

FORT MEYERS BEACH

1.5 hours from Sarasota

Planetary House, Koreshan State Historic Park

Note: The Fort Meyers Beach area is a must-see stop for Florida's best shelling beaches, and is home to a unique, historic religious settlement which I highly recommend visiting.

CAMPING

Koreshan State Historic Park (3800 Corkscrew Rd, Estero) – This unique and peaceful park features the historic Koreshan Settlement, a sizable religious community that thrived in the mid-1890s. Camping amenities include full RV hookups, dump station, laundry and shower facilities. Fees: Tent and RV (40' max length) $26. Book online at www.reserveamerica.com or call (800) 326-3521.

Periwinkle Park and Campground (1119 Periwinkle Way, Sanibel) – This full-service campground and residential park is ideally located on beautiful Sanibel Island, with one of Florida's best shelling beaches only a 10-minute walk away. No pets allowed. Fees: Tent and RV (80' max length) $40-$58 depending on season. E-mail the campground for reservations at periwinklepark@aol.com or call (239) 472-1433.

MUST-SEE ATTRACTIONS

Lover's Key State Park (8700 Estero Blvd, Fort Myers Beach) – This barrier island offers some of the best shelling and outdoor fun in Florida. The two-mile long beach is accessible by boardwalk or tram, and beach supplies (e.g., chairs, umbrellas) are available to rent. Kayak the inner waterways for regular manatee sightings; and bike or hike the five-mile Black Island Trail to view Florida's unique ecology and abundant wildlife. No camping available. Fees: Park entry $8, Bike rental $20 (half day), Kayak rental $38 (half day).

Ding Darling National Wildlife Refuge (900 Tarpon Bay Road, Sanibel) – This wildlife refuge is famous for its large populations of wading birds like white pelicans, roseate spoonbills, ibis, and tricolored herons. The park concessionaire offers guided tram, boat, and kayak tours. Self-guided walking trails and boat, paddleboard, and bike rentals are also available. Don't miss the Visitor and Education Center—one of the best in Florida. Fees: Park entry $5, Nature tours $15-$30, Rentals $10-$35 (hourly).

Koreshan State Historic Park (3800 Corkscrew Rd, Estero) – This beautifully landscaped and unique historic park features the utopian Koreshan Settlement, a religious community that believed that the entire universe existed within a giant, hollow sphere. Most of the buildings are on the National Register of Historic Places. The small, scenic Estero river runs through the park for 3.5 miles to Estero

Bay. Rent a canoe and paddle out to Mound Key Archaeological State Park. You may very well see a manatee along the way.

Captiva Island Beach (14790 Captiva Drive, Captiva) – Just past Sanibel Island lies Captiva Island, its famous shelling beach located on the NW corner of the island. This beach is more remote than Sanibel and has the feel of uncrowded 1960s beach life, with unspoiled sunbathing, shelling, and epic sunsets. Bridge toll required. Dining is available in Captiva town.

THE EVERGLADES

1.5 hrs from Fort Meyers Beach

Mangrove waterway, Everglades National Park

Note: This expansive area includes Big Cypress National Preserve located along Hwy 41 (Tamiami Trail) north of Everglades National Park, and Everglades National Park (mainly situated along SR 9336). Both areas offer must-sees for viewing wildlife by vehicle, foot, or boat; as well as unique camping opportunities. Stop by one of the many Visitor Centers for a supplemental park map.

CAMPING

Midway Campground (Tamiami Trail/Hwy 41, midway between Naples and Miami) – Located within Big Cypress National Preserve, this modest, year-around campground offers 36 full-sized RV and tent sites. All sites are arranged around a small lake. Amenities include electric (no water), dump station, and restrooms. Fees: Tent $24, RV (no length limit) $30.

Trail Lakes Campground (40904 Tamiami Trail/Hwy 41, Ochopee) – Located in Big Cypress National Preserve, this kitschy, privately-owned park, is famous as the headquarters for skunk ape research (Florida's version of Bigfoot). If you ask, the owner will give you a "hands-on" tour of the wildlife exhibit which includes very large snakes, giant scorpions, turtles, a resident alligator, and peacocks. The campground includes 150 full-sized RV and tent sites on 30 acres, as well as charming, thatched-roof chickee cottages. Electric hookups, dump station, Wifi, showers and laundry on-site. Fees: Tent $27.50, RV (no length limit) $33-$44, Chickee Hut $199.

Long Pine Key Campground (Everglades National Park Main Road (Road 9336), seven miles from main park entrance) – This seasonal (Nov 15-April 30), pine-dotted National Park campground offers 108 drive-up sites for tents and RVs (no hookups). Water, dump station, restrooms and showers available. First come, first served. Fees: Tent and RV (36' max length) $20.

MUST-SEE ATTRACTIONS

Big Cypress Bend Boardwalk (27020 Tiamami Trail E, Naples) – A must-see stop along SR 41 (within Fakahatchee Strand State Preserve), this 2,000-foot boardwalk winds through old growth cypress swampland which is considered "the Amazon of Florida". Keep a lookout for the resident bald eagle nest, a popular photo stop.

Everglades National Park Boat Tours (Gulf Coast Visitor Center, 815 Oyster Bar Lane, Everglades City, five miles south of Hwy 41 on SR 29) – For those interested in a narrated boat tour through the islands and inland swamps of Everglades National Park, this should be your first stop. The park concessionaire offers the Mangrove Wilderness and Ten Thousand Lakes tours, as well as canoe and kayak rentals. Tour fees: Adult $37, Child (age 5-12) $19, Boat rentals $28/half day.

Shark Valley Hiking and Biking Trail (Shark Valley Visitor Center, 36000 SW 8th St, Miami, just east of Big Cypress State Preserve on Hwy 41) – Considered the best biking in southern Florida, this 15-mile paved loop trail is a paradise for viewing Everglades ecology and wildlife. The trail ends at an old observation tower, which makes for stunning views. A tram tour is also offered via the Visitor Center.

Wood stork rookery, Big Cypress National Preserve

Anhinga and Gumbo Limbo Trails/ Pa-hay-okee Over-look Trail (Ernest F. Coe Visitor Center, 40001 SR 9336, Homestead) – Popular trails within Everglades National Park, Anhinga and Gumbo Limbo offer guaranteed views of alligators, turtles and various marsh birds (wheelchair accessible). Pa-hay-okee Overlook's observation tower offers an unparalleled, bird's-eye view of the winding Everglades waterways. Nightly ranger walks into alligator country are offered (flashlights available).

Mahogany Hammock Trail (20 miles from Ernest F Coe Visitor Center on SR 9336 (follow signs to trailhead), Everglades National Park) – This half-mile boardwalk winds through freshwater prairie and pineland within Everglades National Park. The canopy is dense and lush (and a little buggy), but it is home to the largest living mahogany tree in the U.S., making it a worthwhile trek deep into the park.

THE FLORIDA KEYS

Key Largo is 2 hours from Everglades City

Key West sunset, Florida

Note: The Florida Keys consists of a long chain of islands once only accessible by water, but now connected by the bridge-dotted Overseas Highway (US 1). The island chain is a coral archipelago—making for wonderful snorkeling, diving, and viewing of marine wildlife. The historic (now defunct) Overseas Railway parallels the Highway, offering interesting photo opportunities. Advanced reservations for State Park and private camping are highly recommended.

CAMPING (Mile markers designated as MM)

John Pennekamp Coral Reef State Park (102601 Overseas Hwy, Key Largo, MM 102.5) – John Pennekamp is an extremely popular, full-service campground with a meager 47 campsites for tents and RVs. Full hookups and modern restrooms with showers; kayak rentals, beach access, and off-shore snorkeling tours offered. Fees: Park entry $8, Tent and RV (55' max length) $38.50. For reservations call (800) 326-3521 or book online at www.reserveamerica.com.

Bahia Honda State Park (36850 Overseas Hwy, Bahia Honda Key, MM 37) – Bahia Honda is located just past the "Middle Keys" and the Seven-Mile Bridge. It offers 80 RV and tent sites, as well as three rustic cabins. The park is famous for its award-winning historic bridge and a lovely snorkeling beach at Florida Bay. Concessions include a gift shop, snack bar, kayak rentals and snorkeling tours to Looe Key National Marine Sanctuary. Fees: Park entry $8, Tent and RV (71' max length) $38.50. For reservations call (800) 326-3521 or book online at www.reserveamerica.com.

Leo's Campground (5236 Suncrest Road, Key West) – Leo's is Key West's smaller, budget-friendly tent and RV campground, very close to the heart of town. The camp-ground is full service, offering waterfront tent camping along a mangrove-lined stream. Notably, there is a pop-ulation of free-roaming iguanas on-site! No pets allowed in tent area. Fees: Tent and RV (42' max length) $44-$78 depending on the season. Reservations can be made by phone at (305) 296-5260.

MUST-SEE ATTRACTIONS

John Pennekamp Coral Reef State Park (US 1, Key Largo, MM 102.5) – This State Park offers some of the best snorkeling and scuba diving in the Keys, as well as glass-bottom boat tours to the surrounding reef. Kayak rentals are available to explore the 50 miles of natural mangrove wilderness trails. Fees: Day use $8; Snorkel tour (2.5 hrs): Adult $29.95, Child $24.95; Kayak rental $12/hr; Glass-bottom boat tour: Adult $24, Child (age 4-11) $17.

African Queen Boat Tours (99701 Overseas Hwy, Key Largo, MM 100) – Humphrey Bogart fans will enjoy this 90-minute cruise on the original, iconic African Queen vessel. Cruise along the Port Largo Canals to the Atlantic and back. Fees: Boat cruise (90 mins) $49; Dinner cruise (2 hrs) $89.

Rain Barrell Artisans Village (86700 Overseas Hwy, Islamorada, MM 86.7) – This colorful, open-air arts and crafts village is famous for its giant (30-foot-high, 40-foot-long), picture-worthy lobster named Betsy. The souvenir shopping is also excellent and budget-friendly.

National Key Deer Refuge Visitor Center (179 Key Deer Blvd, Big Pine Key, MM 30) – This Visitor Center offers excellent wildlife viewing from its observation deck, and it is worthwhile to hike one of the many nature trails throughout the Refuge. Most notably, the endangered key deer (a miniature deer species) is found only here in the Keys. Note: a short drive through the residential No Name Key (1/2 mile west of Big Pine Key at Mile Marker 35) may afford you an additional glimpse of the resident key deer.

Bahia Honda State Park (36850 Overseas Highway, Bahia Honda, MM 37) – Bahia Honda is famous for its award-winning, historic bridge (with amazing views) and a lovely snorkeling beach at Florida Bay. Manta rays are common here. The park concessionaire offers kayak rentals and snorkeling tours to the pristine Looe Key National Marine Sanctuary (great for novice snorkelers). Fees: Park entry $8; Snorkel tour: Adult $29.95,   Child $24.95; Kayak rental $12/hr.

Key West Attractions (US 1, MM 0) – Key West lies at the end of the Overseas Hwy and is the quintessential Keys experience. Some notable Must-See Attractions include:

- **Duval Street** (wander the historic neighborhoods by foot); **Mallory Square** (famous for its lively street scene and sunsets);

- **Historic Key West Seaport** (excellent for scenic walks along the harbor and a great location for dinner);

- **Zachary Taylor Historic State Park** (Take a ranger-led tour of the Fort and its large collection of Civil War-era cannons, snorkel the live coral reef, and watch the sunset crowd-free. Fees: Day use $8, Snorkel gear $20); and

- **West Martello Tower** (This incomplete Civil War-era fort is a hidden gem and a National Historic Site, with lush botanical gardens throughout, and an historic African slave cemetery on the grounds. Don't miss this unique, free attraction—a local favorite.)

***

I hope the culmination of this travel guide finds you satisfied and full of amazing memories. When you decide to take another road trip adventure, you will find the following soon-to-be completed travel guides will make your journey up the coastline or throughout the majestic western states as seamless as possible:

Kim's Travel Guide for RV and Tent Camping in the USA
West Coast Route: California, Oregon and Washington

and

Kim's Travel Guide for RV and Tent Camping in the USA
Western Parks Loop: CA, AZ, NM, CO, WY, and MT

Kimberly Wiedemeier has over 25 years of domestic and international travel experience under her proverbial pack. Her education includes a B.S. in Biology and an M.A. in Anthropology. Her true passion is travel, and she especially enjoys finding (and sharing) hidden gems that are off the beaten path. When she is not traveling in her camper she enjoys hosting international guests in her California home, as well as spending quality time with her husband and robot-loving son.

If you would like to contact me, I'd love to hear from you via email at kimstravelguide@gmail.com. I am also available to create custom travel itineraries (locally and around the world) for a reasonable fee (website coming soon).